Erna,

My teacher, sent to me
from our Divine Master Teacher, who
You have so much to give from the
very essence of who you are. God
implanted you with the knowledge & wi
to complete your assignment —
Bountiful Blessings &
Evelyn Dumas 8/4/09

Writings From The Well-Spring Of My Soul

Inspirational Poems of Faith and Restoration

A Journey To Healing And Restoration

By

Evelyn Dumas' Chavez

1663 Liberty Drive, Suite 200
Bloomington, Indiana 47403
(800) 839-8640
www.authorhouse.com

First published by AuthorHouse 05/18/04

ISBN: 1-4184-3413-2 (sc)

Library of Congress Control Number:2004105308

Printed in the United States of America
Bloomington, Indiana

This book is printed on acid-free paper.

Table of Contents

Acknowledgements

I must thank God first for inspiring me in a special way that remains an absolute mystery to me. I thank God for speaking to my heart so I could hear him.

I have always had a passion for writing letters of comfort to family and friends, but I never knew there was anything else buried within me. I have always loved people and had a burning desire to help improve the quality of life for someone other than my family and me. No one could have told me that I would be writing anything other than letters.

I give special thanks to my beloved children, Stanley, Celestine, Steven, Catrina and my grand children. I also thank my Massage Therapist, my sisters, my husband (who created a lot of drama in my life) and all of the ladies I have worked with daily who encouraged me when I felt like I could not write for anyone other than me.

I am grateful for everything that has been done through me and to me. I am thankful for all of life's many lessons. I count it all joy. Had it not been for the trials in my life, The Well-Spring of My Soul would not have overflowed.

By Evelyn Dumas' Chavez

THIS BOOK IS DEDICATED TO THE MEMORY OF MY PARENTS

THE LATE

MATTIE CUNNINGHAM DUMAS'

AND

THE LATE

EUGENE ALBERT DUMAS' SR.

During their lifetime they gave me the gift that kept on giving. They introduced me to my Lord and Savior Jesus Christ. I will be eternally grateful to them for teaching me to love everyone no matter who they are or where they came from.

"A Journey to the Under World"

There is no other way to phrase it, other than a bad dream.

Most of the players were from another realm it seemed.

This all started with a call from someone I did not consider a friend.

The voice on the line vanished, then my journey began.

I found myself to be a spectator in another realm and time.

What I witnessed has remained imprinted in my mind.

I was high and lifted up with a heavenly being in the sky.

There was a man bound on an altar with many demons standing by.

I cried out to the man, you must start praying!

He lay there motionless, like he could not hear a word I was saying.

I screamed out, Oh God please don't let him die!

I screamed again and again you must pray, at least try.

The ground began to quake and the chains that bound him began to break.

I was told that it was by deception that the man had come to a place of no hope.

Now I know that angels named Grace and Mercy are the ones who cast out salvation's rope.

+

Submit yourselves therefore to God. Resist the devil,
and he will flee from you.
Draw nigh to God, and He will draw nigh to you. Cleanse your hands, ye sinners; and purify your hearts, ye double minded. James 4:7-8 KJV

A Time for Rejoicing

A time for rejoicing brings great pleasure.

This time gives birth to memories that will be treasured.

We often rejoice when one is born, but never when one dies.

We forget that death gives way to a new beginning; so we ask why as we cry.

Grief causes one to forget that death is not the end;

We are given a glorified body then new life begins.

There is no sickness or sorrow or need for medication.

We enter the Garden called Beautiful; a heavenly creation.

The Garden called Beautiful is in another realm and time.

There is no sadness or sorrow; only absolute peace of mind.

A time of rejoicing will begin when my spirit takes wings and fly.

Please remember I have gone back to the giver of all life; I did not die.

To enter the Garden called Beautiful you must trust and believe;

It is yours for the asking; open your heart and receive.

Please remember as you face the dawning of a new day;

Jesus is the answer; He is the only way!

Jesus said unto her, "I am the resurrection and the life: he that believeth in Me, though he were dead, yet shall he live: (26 And whosoever liveth and believeth in Me shall never die. Believest thou this?" John 11: 25-26 KJV

A Trip Down Memory Lane

We live in a world of constant change,

Very few, if any thing remains the same.

In times like these I realize that I am alone,

I find myself revisiting pleasant times that are past and gone.

I sometimes think how things have changed,

I would like to stroll down memory lane.

Where is memory lane one might ask?

It may be in some boxes, in an attic or lost in the past.

As you grow older, you no longer play.

You may sit and yearn for yesterday.

You talk about the way things used to be,

You revisit your past where you feel at ease.

Memory Lane is in the distant past,

Your journey there is brief, it cannot last.

The only way for you to be content,

Is to remember the visit is free, it doesn't cost one cent!

Inspired by those who journey to Memory Lane

A War Torn World

Last night I lay in bed fast asleep,

Visions of a war torn world began to seep.

I saw a world ravaged by the horrors of war,

I asked myself… what is war good for?

The world as we've known it had become a desolate place,

Hate and discontent had destroyed the human race.

War is not part of God's original plan,

Death and greed came into the world because of disobedience by man.

Submission to God is a must for everyone,

The only way to the Father, is by his Son.

Then our world would become a better place,

Hate and bitterness would cease among every race.

Then terrors of war would no longer be a reality,

There would be no remnants of war for anyone to see.

And ye shall hear of wars and rumours of wars: see that ye are not troubled: for all these things must come to pass, but the end is not yet. (7For nation shall rise against nation and kingdom against kingdom; and there shall be famines, pestilences, and earthquakes in divers places. (8 All these are the beginning of sorrows. Matthew 24: 6-8 KJV

“Accepting Change”

It is too easy to remain the same.

You can hold on to the past and not change.

We hold onto our wounds like battle scars or constant friends.

If they are released or forgiven, change begins.

You say that you want the pain to go away.

Yet you revisit your pain everyday.

Pain is like a flower; it will grow if you feed it.

Stop cultivating and caring for it; the growth quits!

Accepting change is very hard,

Start seeing yourself differently for a start.

You must have a dream and a scheme for your life.

Change is inevitable even though there is pain and strife.

“Judge not, and ye shall not be judged: condemn not, and ye shall not be condemned: forgive, and ye shall be forgiven. (37 Give, and it shall be given unto you: good measure, pressed down shaken together, and running over, shall men give into your bosom. For with the same measure that ye mete withal it shall be measured to you again. Luke 6:37-38 KJV

Being Tried By God

When life circumstances start to shift,

You become acutely aware that you have been adrift.

You have strayed so far away from God,

That the sifting and trying of your soul begins to start.

Then you cried out to God, "please, rescue me?

This pain is too great; I want some relief."

You must get down on your knees to pray,

Then ask the Comforter to show you the way.

Know that God is allowing this to happen to you,

You'll become stronger because of what you are going through.

So never sit for long and cry why me?

This is a refining process that will set you free.

The trial first starts in the mind,

With tormenting words that are unkind.

Sometimes terrible things may happen to you,

But God will give you beauty for ashes and bring you through.

It is by grace that you endure Being Tried By God,

The gift that you receive will be a change of heart.

The Spirit of the Lord God is upon Me; because the Lord hath anointed Me To preach good tidings unto the meek; He hath sent Me to bind up the brokenhearted, to proclaim liberty to the captives, and the opening of the prison to them that are bound; 2] To proclaim the acceptable year of the Lord, and the day of vengeance of our God; to comfort all that mourn, 3] To appoint unto them that mourn in Zion, to give onto them beauty for ashes, the oil of praise for the spirit of heaviness; that they might be called trees of righteousness, the planting of the Lord, that He might be glorified.

Isaiah 61:1-3 KJV

Bitterness Takes Its' Toll

Haven't I always been there for you?

Can you please explain why you do the things you do?

I must tell you bitterness always takes its' toll,

It doesn't matter if you are young or old.

Of course, I know this is not about me anyway,

So it doesn't matter what I do or say.

You constantly blame others for all the obstacles in your life,

The harder you try to hurt others; the more you are bombarded by strife.

You have become so angry, bitter and cold over time,

No one can enter the prison that you created in your mind.

You have deceived yourself into thinking you are right,

You are now walking in darkness; there is no light.

Somewhere along the way you crossed the line,

You decided that evil doing would give you peace of mind.

But instead, you became a tormented soul,

That allowed hostility and bitterness to take control.

Hostility and bitterness has taken its' toll,

You have made hurting others your only goal.

Will you choose life today?

Stop hurting others; begin to pray.

You must repent and turn to God,

Then ask God to create in you a new heart.

Grace and Mercy will come right in,

After there is true repentance, restoration begins.

You have a chance to begin again,

But only you can turn from your sins.

Repentance and restoration must become your goal,

Then bitterness and hostility can no longer take root in your soul.

Rest in the Lord, and wait patiently for Him: fret not thyself because of him who prospereth in his way, because of the man who bringeth wicked devices to pass. 8] Cease from anger, and forsake wrath: fret not thyself in any wise to do evil. 9] For evildoers shall be cut off: but those that wait upon the Lord, they shall inherit the earth. Psalm 37:7-9 KJV

Broken Treasures

Inspired by a broken crystal bowl from my son

Crystal bowls, diamond rings and Tiffany glass,

Robbers steal or we break, they may not last.

A gift from the heart is treasured.

The heart's intent is how a treasure is measured.

The treasures we receive and value over the years,

If they are stolen or broken bring heartaches and tears.

On the day we open our treasure we say, this gift we will hold dear.

We never consider that the loss of this treasure will bring heartaches and tears.

A true treasure can never be replaced and money cannot buy.

You will cherish it and all the memories it gives you until you die.

I have been told that there are eternal treasures that are in another place where we live forever!

I asked if robbers could steal them or they could be destroyed; I was told no. Never!

But my God shall supply all your needs according to His riches in glory by Jesus Christ. Philippians 4:19 KJV

"Broken Trust"

Once trust is broken it is hard to regain,

Your mind replays the hurt and all the pain!

There are restless days and sleepless nights,

You try to forgive and do what is right!

The hurt you feel can make the heart turn cold,

Then you begin the battle for your soul.

For as you know forgiveness is a must,

I must confess it is now hard to trust.

Now you look to heaven and say,

Lord, please make this pain go away!

I know I cannot keep this hurt inside.

I must forgive and forget false pride.

Broken trust can be restored someday,

True forgiveness is the only way.

Bless the Lord, O my soul, and all that is within me, bless His holy name. 2] Bless the Lord O my soul, and forget not all His benefits: 3] Who forgiveth all thine iniquities; who healeth all thy diseases.
Psalm 103:1-3 KJV

Can You Take Fire To Your Bosom And Not Be Burned?

This is a mystery that is ages old.

It is through life experiences the riddle unfolds.

You look at the riddle and you wonder what does it mean?

The thought of fire burning you makes you scream!

This question is not applicable to our lives you may say.

It is dismissed as an outdated bible saying any way.

The thought of fire to your chest really makes you scream!

You think, the only way it would happen is in a bad dream.

This is not really about fire; it is about deception and betrayed trust.

It started in the Garden when Abel's blood cried out from the dust.

An enemy cannot hurt you like the ones you love and trust to the end.

The pain is greater if betrayal is by a loved one or friend.

Betrayal and deception by those we trust and love causes us such pain,

So much is lost and nothing is gained!

So, can you take fire to your bosom and not be burned?

There are greater lessons from life that you must learn.

Misplaced confidence creates heartbreaks and stress.

We must depend more on God and from man, expect less.

We start out with good intent,

Then in the end you wonder where it went.

There are some things that should never be spoken to man.

He will distort what you say and cause you pain.

If you have a problem you want to share.

Take it to the Lord, He really cares.

After all, there is nothing man can really do,

Give the problem to the Lord, He will see you through.

Crying During The Night

As I cried out to the Lord Speak to me,

I could hear His voice whisper oh so sweetly.

Child you have been calling me for so long,

Telling me about all the things you have done wrong.

You were crying and talking so loud that you could not hear,

That I said, “I heard you; I bottled all your tears”.

I heard every prayer that you prayed,

I came to comfort you; don’t be afraid.

I will dry all your tears,

I came that you might be delivered from your fears.

Just find comfort in knowing that I heard you Crying During The Night.

My child don’t worry, everything is going to be all right.

I have been with you even before your life began,

Just reach out for me; I will hold your hand.

You never have to be overcome by fear,

Just remember that your Heavenly Father is always near.

The Lord is my strength and song, and He is become my salvation: He is my God, and I will prepare him am habitation; my father’s God, and I will exalt Him. Exodus 15:2 KJV

Do Not Weep for Me

When I left, I fell asleep,

For me my love, You should not weep!

I know you were not ready for me to go.

My journey came to an end, as you must know.

I tried to stay; I did not want to leave.

I had just found love; I knew your heart would bleed.

I am in a beautiful place where there is no pain.

The sun always shines there is no rain.

Please, do not weep for me!

I am not dead; I just fell asleep.

As you must know, God had a better plan.

God has restored my body. I am a new man.

I will walk in the garden called Beautiful everyday.

I know we will meet again if you keep the faith and pray.

Please do not weep for me long.

The Comforter will restore your peace and make you strong.

My life was short, but our love was grand!

We will meet again to live and love in this new land.

So, do not weep for me I say!

We will meet again someday.

Inspired by my nephew The Late Raymond Lawson Candelaria

Do You Bother Me?

Do you bother me? Don't you know?

It never mattered if you bothered me before.

What does bother mean to you?

You know the answer, to thy own self be true.

You are at a stage in your life,

Any answer I give you can cause you strife!

Why should I do this to myself?

You spent all your wonder years with someone else.

Do you bother me?

Do you want the truth or a lie?

I will ponder my response before telling you why.

As I lay and burn in my bed;

My longings and desires were never fed.

Now in the winter of your life you say,

Do I bother you today?

My response, Oh no my dear,

No way!

As I lay on my bed contemplating a response that was cutting, a soft voice spoke to me from the Essence of my Soul. The voice whispered words of compassion, then I began to pray. Lord I thank you for loving me in a special way. Letting me feel loved, even though I feel like there is no love in my home. I thank you for being with me, even though I feel so alone. And I thank you most of all for turning my nights into day and taking the sting of betrayal and disappointment away. Lord, I want to praise you for being my everything. With the dawning of each new day I am renewed like a breath of spring. Thank you for keeping my feet from running to do wrong. And I thank you for giving me strength to go on. You promised in your word that you would provide a means of escape. So, I thank you for keeping me during the times I experienced so much heartbreak. Amen.

"Do You Know Me"?

As I lay in my bed,
A million thoughts go through my head.
I look at the reflection in the mirror,
Yet the mystery of who I am is no clearer.
Do you know me I say?
You look at me and walk away.
So I ask myself how can this be?
I now realize, you do not know me.
Now the mystery causes me to be afraid,
As many thoughts go through my head.
I sit in despair and begin to cry,
I wonder to myself, Who am I?
Have you seem me before?
Do you know me? I want to know.
Could I have lived in another place and time?
A million thoughts keep flooding my mind.
As I lay in my bed,
The question replays in my head.
The search is over now someone responded,
You are free and no longer in bondage.

Inspired by Devin

"Don't Be Afraid"

When you are afraid the flame of hope grows dim.

Look to your maker and trust in Him.

We constantly ask God to do His part,

Before He can work, you must let him into your heart.

There is a price that we must pay,

Just say to the Lord, have thy own way!

Don't be afraid to trust in God,

He will give you hope for tomorrow… for a start.

When the trials of life make you feel grim,

Don't be afraid to trust in Him!

There is no fear in love; but perfect love casteth out fear: because fear hath torment. He that feareth is not made perfect in love. 1 John 4:17 KJV

"Don't Be Sad My Child"!

Don't be sad my child,

Everything will be okay after a while.

Let your mind be free of life's cares,

There will be no burden too hard for you to bear.

Let the tears fall freely from your face,

The hurt and pain will leave without a trace.

There is a bright side to this dark cloud,

Just lift your voice and sing out loud.

I am sure that this is so,

Because I have walked where you are walking before,

I can understand your sadness and pain,

But the sun always shines after the rain.

Don't be sad my child I say,

I know the Lord will make a way!

Hold your head up and see,

A radiant smile and hope brings victory!

Inspired by my daughter Celestine

Don't Judge Me

Don't judge me, I am free!

The price was paid on Calvary.

Forget the person I used to be,

I have been forgiven I am free.

Don't hold on to my past,

I will not, I am free at last!

I will live forgiven everyday,

I thank God as I pray.

So, don't judge me, I am free.

I am not the person I used to be.

I will not be a prisoner of my past,

I have a new song, Free at last!

"Don't Let Hate Enter In"

Don't let hate enter in,

You will wonder where and when it began.

It will take on a life force of it's own,

With every new day it will get strong.

Hate consumes the person you used to be.

Hate has taken your liberty!

Don't let hate enter in,

Hate is from the deceiver; hate is not your friend.

Hate takes hold quickly, but it is not to late.

You can change this terrible fate.

Break the chains that shackle your mind,

You can be free. Just be kind.

You can sing and rejoice!

Knowing that you have made the right choice.

Never let hate enter in,

Hate is a deceiver; hate is not your friend.

"Don't Let Love Pass You By"

Don't let love pass you by,

You'll look back and wonder why.

Love is like nectar in a beautiful glass,

Savor it slowly, make it last!

Love is like the warm sunshine after a cold rain,

It quickens the inner soul to live again!

Savor every moment and the joy it brings,

Say goodbye to the winter in your life and say hello to spring.

Don't let love pass you by,

There will be no need to look back and wonder why.

Love is more than beauty in a glass,

Love is eternal, true love last!

Inspired by my sister Bessie

"Don't Misuse My Love For You"

Don't misuse my love for you.

It will break my heart if you do.

You asked me to forgive you again and again.

Without true repentance you remain the same.

A heart unchanged is without the Savior,

It is evidenced by the same old behaviors!

An unchanged heart is very cold.

It puts you in the midst of a battle for your soul!

You don't even know, you are not aware,

Your heart is very cold and you don't even care.

Don't misuse my love is my constant plea.

I began to pray for the shackles to be released.

The tears I have shed fell on the throne of mercy and grace.

All the pain and heartache I felt will leave without a trace.

For a brief moment you can see the light of day.

You realize you have been blind and have lost your way.

You asked the Savior for forgiveness for a start,

Then you repented and asked God to heal your heart.

"Don't Sell Out"!

When you sell your soul;

You become evil, angry and cold.

You become a sower that sows to the wind,

Then you reap a full harvest of what seems to be good in a whirlwind.

Your journey into a world of deception and power begins.

It doesn't matter who you hurt, your family or your friends.

You keep telling yourself, you are the best!

This is your journey up the ladder of success.

The higher you climb your heart turns cold.

You have unknowingly entered a deal for your soul.

You feel more empowered day after day,

You are now successful and you no longer pray.

Who needs God you begin to say?

You shout, I have the world on a string! A voice whispers no way!

You have entered a world that is dark and cold.

Over the entrance is a sign the battle for your soul.

Now you are alone and you begin to cry!

Save me Jesus, I don't want to die!

If you save me and set me free;

I will serve you for all eternity!

Please Jesus, hear my prayer;

Your soul cries out in despair.

Before the prayer was finished the earth began to shake,

The chains that held you bound began to break.

You then began to realize selling out was not wise.

Your only goal now is to seek the eternal prize.

The road you now walk, you sometimes feel alone.

Your idea of success now is to make heaven your home.

Inspired by those who sold out to the idea of success

From The Well Spring of My Soul

From the wellspring of my soul,

Life long secrets begin to unfold.

Stories that were once buried deep,

Given to the subconscious mind to keep.

Now when I lay down to sleep,

Life time memories begin to seep.

Life long mysteries start to unwind.

When did I live in this place or time?

Why is this place and people coming to my mind?

I'll keep on searching until the answers I'll find.

Their faces and costumes seem so familiar to me.

I joined in with them so eagerly.

I thought I saw my brother at a gathering.

The man told me that I did not really know him.

Who was that man? He was very bold.

I guess he is one of my life mysteries From The Well Spring of My Soul!

A Dream

Give God Your All

Even though your life seems so full of stress,

You constantly try to do your best.

Then all of a sudden, you heard a voice calling out to you,

You asked, is it you Lord; what shall I do?

You are tired and weary for lack of rest,

You hear another voice say; your life is in a mess.

You can be proud that you've done your best,

Yet you know in your heart this is another test.

Following the ways of the world will make you fall,

God is still calling and He wants your all.

You cannot walk with God and satisfy your flesh,

God wants all of you; not just your best!

No man can serve two masters: for either he will hate the one, and love the other; or else he will hold to the one, and despise the other. Ye cannot serve God and mammon. Matthew 6:24 KJV

God Created You For More

You have been feeling down even more than before,

You know that your life has a greater purpose, your heart wants to soar.

You must not listen to the negative statements you hear everyday,

You know that you can overcome if you change your ways.

Surely God has created you for much more,

Like the eagle that thought he was a chicken; you will begin to soar.

There was a time when your self-esteem was at an all time low,

You stop using your imagination and could no longer grow.

When you lose your imagination; you no longer dream,

You're trapped in a self destructive pattern with no way out it seems.

You are God's creation; the one that He adores,

Always remember that God Created You for More.

He brought me up also out of an horrible pit, out of the miry clay, and set my feet upon a rock, and established my goings. 3] And He hath put a new song in my mouth, even praise unto our God: many shall see it, and fear, and shall trust in the Lord. Psalm 40:2-3 KJV

God Has A Blessing For You

During these times you think about the things you have gone through,

Be of good courage, God has a blessing for you.

I know that you think you have suffered in vain,

But just stand up and tell the world you would gladly go through it again.

Let me tell you, it was all part of God's Master Plan,

You must run your race with valor and when it's over; just stand.

God Has A Blessing For You,

You were not alone when you were suffering; He was there too.

He was the one, who eased all your pain,

When He touched you, no pain could remain.

God wants to bless you in a special way,

So just run swiftly to Him and kneel to pray.

Be of good courage your suffering has come to an end,

God has restored you; you won't have to go through it again.

He understands everything that happened that made you blue,

I am here to tell you, God Has A Blessing For You.

So don't worry about what people may do or say,

Just stand! Receive your blessings today!

Heaven Is On My Mind

I woke up this morning to the bright sunshine,

I thought about unconditional love that is by heaven's design.

I could not help but think about all the things God has done for me,

Then I thought about His ultimate sacrifice on a hill called Calvary.

I had to remind myself, "He died so I could live".

Then I had to ask myself, "is there anything I can give"?

What can I give to God for such an act of love?

When He died on the cross, it was me He was thinking of.

I fell to my knees to pray for understanding,

Then He revealed that He wanted a heart that is not demanding.

I'll give Him a contrite heart, one that is broken and kind,

Then I'll rejoice as I go through the day with heaven on my mind.

I Call Jesus When I Fall

When my days are hard and my nights are long,

I feel battered and beaten by life's storms.

I call on Jesus because He is always near,

He heals my broken heart and dries all my tears!

There are no mountains that are too high to climb,

I call on Jesus for assurance and peace of mind.

When life situations fill my heart with fear,

I have the calm assurance that Jesus is always near.

I go to Him in secret prayer,

I can leave all my burdens and heartaches there.

It is so wonderful just to know that I have a friend,

That knew all about me before my life began.

As I lay on my bed to sleep,

He will keep me in perfect peace.

After all,

I call on Jesus when I fall.

Blessed is the man that trusteth in the Lord, and whose hope the Lord is.
Jeremiah 17:7 KJV

"I Can't Complain"

No two days and nights are ever the same.

One brings happiness the next brings pain.

I must confess that I know I am blest.

At the close of the day I can lay my head on my pillow and rest.

When I awake and see that the skies are cloudy and it is raining;

I say to my soul there is no reason to start complaining.

I can't complain will be my song of praise,

As I look toward heaven this hymn I'll raise!

For sun shiny days or cold rainy nights,

I will not complain, God knows what is right.

So, before I inventory the day and start to stress;

I will remind myself that I have been blest!

Inspired by my son Steven

"I Don't Want To Face The Day"

I awake early, at the break of day;

I get on my knees and begin to pray.

Lord, I don't want to face the day.

Please strengthen me to do your will anyway!

There are so many situations that cause disdain,

Loved ones pierce my heart and I cry out in pain!

Lord, please! How can this be?

These trying situations keep troubling me.

I look out the window, the sky is gray.

I get back down on my knees and begin to say;

Lord, I don't want to face the day.

I am tired of working, but I must go anyway.

I know that I'm in bondage and I want to be free;

I'll keep asking the Comforter to rescue me.

As I keep praying, I feel my burdens fade away.

Now I see a ray of hope in this new day!

I Felt The Master's Touch

The day God touched me; I was set free.

The pain from my past could no longer hinder me.

My heart was fixed; I lost the desire to complain,

I turned away from the world for heaven's gain.

I knew in my heart that God had a plan for me,

Now the dainties of the world had become a fading memory.

The things that once gave me immense pleasure,

I am now willing to relinquish for eternal treasure.

For God alone will comfort and keep me,

He loosed the shackles and set me free.

My life as I had lived it was forever changed,

The night I felt the Master's hands.

There is one thing that will always mean so much,

Just knowing that I Felt The Master's Touch.

Truly my soul silently waiteth upon God: from Him comes my salvation. 2] He only is my rock and my salvation; He is my defence; I shall not be greatly moved. Psalm 62:1-2 KJV

I Must Answer The Call

There shall come a time and a day,

I will feel homeward bound and I'll fly away.

I'll say goodbye to my family and my friends,

My journey here will be over and new life shall begin.

My forefathers spoke of a Beautiful Garden full of many wonderful things,

It is a place of absolute peace and the angels sing.

The garden's pathways are paved with pure gold,

The leaves on the trees can be used for healing all weary souls.

On my journey, I called Jesus whenever I would fall.

I am now being summoned and I must answer the call.

I can hear someone singing two wings to fly away,

Even though I am homeward bound I must work on earth until I go home to stay.

Answering the call means I must first die to my flesh,

Then I will be worthy to do God's will because I've become less.

I can no longer ignore the voice that is calling out to me,

I Must Answer The Call then I will be set free.

I Never Said Goodbye

I never had the chance to say goodbye,

You were going for a ride, I did not know you would die.

I remember waiting for you to come home,

It was just like yesterday that I heard the ringing of the phone.

The voice that I heard was not familiar to me,

It was the Bearer of Bad News, telling me of the tragedy.

The dart of death had pierced your heart,

Now my world as I had known it was torn apart.

It seemed like a horrible storm that would not end,

I would not ever be able to talk to you again.

I could get angry and ask God why,

But I know He knew the very day you would die.

I truly believe He knew all about us before our birth,

I also believe our days are numbered here on earth.

I can only thank Him for allowing you to be a part of my life,

Knowing that you gave me great joy and pleasure sprinkled with some strife.

Now I must face this dreaded day,

I must say Goodbye; you've gone away.

I know this is not the end,

I have faith in God; we shall meet again.

Now He that hath wrought us for the selfsame thing is God, who also hath given us the earnest of the Spirit. 6] Therefore we are always confident, knowing that, whilst we are at home in the body, we are absent from the Lord. 7](For we walk by faith, not by sight: 8]
We are confident, I say, and willing rather to be absent from the body, and to be present with the Lord. 2 Corinthians 5:5-8 KJV

I Still Hear Mama Praying

In Honor of The Gal

I can still hear mama praying when she bowed down on her knees,
The doors of heaven were opened by her fervent prayers and pleas.
Lord, will you hide my children in the shelter of your arms?
Please protect and keep each one of them from all anxiety and harm.
I can still hear her praying, please Lord open their ears and eyes,
Don't let them be misled by satan's deception and lies.
Please lead and guide them safely along the way,
Speak to their hearts my loving Savior each and everyday.
Lord, I am trusting in your promises, as I give my precious children to you,
Please open their hearts so they will know that your words are true.
I Still Hear Mama Praying even though she has passed away.
I like mama am asking you to bless and keep my children every day.

It is Your Season

Our lives are in tune with the rhythm of the earth,

All that we do was predestined long before our birth.

With this in mind our lives are part of a grand scheme.

We have freedom to choose to live out our dreams.

The path we take may take us on a detour,

That detour may lead to more pain and sorrow than we want to endure.

With stress and strain there come a few lessons,

We should listen to the voice that guides us in a positive direction.

There is a divine purpose for everything and a reason.

If you believe in divine purpose, you now understand life's seasons.

Inspired by my sister Carrie

"It's Me Lord"!

Lord it's me again!

I have been forsaken by those I called my friends.

I had to tell you today,

I am open now, have thy own way!

I have been through the fire and the flood,

You have saved my soul with your blood.

You have been changing me with the trials of life.

I can now give thanks for pain and strife.

Lord it is me, calling again,

I want you to bless those I call my friends.

Let them know this is not the end,

You are our Father and eternal friend.

Please bless them in a special way.

Give them hope to face a brand new day!

It's Praying Time

Whenever I am unable to sleep,

I know it's time for the Lord to speak.

I get on my knees and begin to pray,

I want to hear what the Lord has to say.

Now I know It's Praying Time,

Its time for me to do the Lord's will not mine.

I have had plenty time to tell Him about my needs,

Now it's time for me to take heed.

I started out the day asking the Lord to speak to my heart,

Now I must listen so He will not depart.

I must be still so I can hear every word that He has to say,

I just want to do His will as I go through each day.

So whenever I 'm awakened in the middle of the night, that's fine,

I know in my heart that It's Praying Time.

If ever there is a time when you cannot sleep,

Just get on your knees and ask the Lord to speak.

Just make up your mind to listen so you can hear,

He will speak to you in ways that are very clear.

You must know that He will speak to you throughout the day,

You must be obedient or He will go away.

So whenever I cannot sleep, I don't mind,

I know without a doubt; It's Praying Time.

It's Your Time

This is the time when you feel free from the pain of your past.

Your soul cries out, It's your time at last!

You have wandered through life with no direction,

Making you vulnerable, without any protection.

You inventory your life and you do not like where you are.

You have no home; you live in your car!

You can hear a soft voice say,

Be of good courage, God will make a way.

You wake up in the morning and see the bright sunshine,

You keep telling yourself, life has been kind.

So many plans and schemes replay in your head,

You try hard to forget every negative thing you have said.

The words whispered by a soft voice begin to chime,

Hold your head up, keep the faith. It's your time!

Inspired by the Homeless

Jesus Are You There?

When your heart has been broken and it seems no one cares,

Your soul cries out to heaven, Jesus are You there?

You need someone to talk to but your friends cannot be found,

You sit alone and cry until there is no sound.

Again your soul cries out, Jesus are You there?

I am so heavy laden; I wonder if You care.

With the dawning of each new day the tears begin to fall,

You shouted Jesus! I know You hear me, please answer my call.

You feel forsaken by your family and your friends,

It seems that they abandoned you, when your troubles began.

You are broken and battered by the trials of life.

Inner healing must begin to rid your soul of strife

You have entered a place and time for spiritual restoration.

You must be willing to be restored; then become a new creation.

Jesus, are You there? Will no longer be your call,

You now know that Jesus was with you after all!

**For the Lord God is a sun and shield: The Lord will give grace and glory: no good thing will he withhold from them that walk uprightly.
Psalms 84:11 KJV

Jesus May I Talk to You?

Jesus I need a friend in whom I can confide.

I have all these problems I cannot keep inside.

I need someone to talk to who will listen to what I say.

Someone, who will not tell me, resolve the problem this way.

I'd like to talk to my loved ones but they have problems of their own.

I cannot find resolution and I cannot bear these burdens alone.

Jesus may I talk to you while I'm on my knees.

Please lift my burdens and grant me some peace.

I know that you will hear me no matter what I say.

Please come into my heart now dear Lord, have thy own way.

Having this talk with you has given me such relief.

I just want to thank you for giving me perfect peace.

Jesus, The Sacrificial Offering

When I see a rushing stream,

I think of God's majesty on a grander scheme.

God in all of his awesome power,

Created the streams and brooks in less than an hour.

He divided the land from the sea,

He hung the moon, stars and sun in the sky to provide light for eternity.

I am talking about the Mighty God who separated night from day,

Then he created man out of dirt and clay.

He said, "man should not be alone,

Then created woman from man's bone".

He gave them a beautiful garden to live in,

Until they committed the very first sin.

Fruit from the tree of knowledge opened their eyes,

They knew that they were naked, so they tried to hide.

Life in Paradise had come to an end,

Adam and Eve had committed a sin.

Eden could not be home anymore,

They were out casts; they had to go.

Eve gave birth to babies while Adam put his hands to the plow,

In the end everyone would surely live and die.

Now that sin entered into the world there would be travail and outcries.

Because of the serpent's deception there would be death and more lies.

By reason of sin, there needed to be a way for man to be saved,

God sent his only son who was crucified and rose from the grave.
It was The Precious Lamb of God, who shed his blood on the cross,
Jesus was the ultimate sacrificial offering who died and rose again so a sin
sick world would not be lost.

Life's Longings

Life's longings are never to be fulfilled. We long for so many things during our lifetime. We long for love, fortune and fame, the things very few attain. We search our entire life, trying to fill an emptiness that only God can fill. We look for the love that is never to be found because we start our search without God.

We pour out of ourselves until we are empty and in despair and we feel no one cares. We orchestrate our own misery by failing to seek God's will for our lives. We start out in the flesh, seeking what we want and not God's will for our lives and we wonder why we fail. We have but to see who is the captain of our ship and maybe we will face reality. If God is not at the center of our every effort, then we are shipwrecked; lost on the sea of life.
When we find ourselves lost at sea in the trials of life, we cry why me? What have I done to deserve this evil? Please Jesus, deliver me from all my troubles. We cannot look inside of ourselves to see that at the center our soul is a river called despair. It is full of the things we want to feed our flesh on until we are fat.

We then begin to pray as if God is Santa Claus and we give Him our Christmas list. And the terrors of life continue. We are not shaken to reality yet. We continue to pray for things that will never fill our emptiness. We still believe that if we had one more thing we would feel better and we would not feel alone and sad. We will be Happy! Oh happy, happy! Joy! Joy! Love and happiness cannot be found in things that money can buy or the passions of the heart.

It is written that we have not, because we ask not. So, the prayers reach the throne of grace and mercy and Jesus gives us the things we ask for.
One day we wake up to so many things that we have collected on our journey and we find, we are still empty, sad and lonely. We still have nothing, no love to call our own. We then reach out to share our life with someone who understands the pain of loneliness, only to be betrayed. Betrayal takes one to the very pits of hell. Then and only then do you sincerely cry out to your maker, The Lord Jesus Christ. We ask for mercy, but in our despair, we also ask why. Why me? What have I done to deserve this evil? Jesus! Save me! Please?

We have come to the hour of darkness in our lives and we are lost without the light of God. We wonder why we cannot see.

We cannot remember when we fell into this dark place. For it was by deception that we fell. We were following the desires of our heart without guidance from The Comforter. The angel of darkness whispered and we followed the sound without seeing where we were going. He said, come to this Garden called Beautiful. It is full of wonderful things and you will be happy there. We ran blindly, without knowing where we were going or how long it would take to get to our destination. And before we knew it, we were no longer children running and playing, we were young adults trying to make it. During this season we were so full of ourselves until we did not think about tomorrow. After all, we just wanted to have fun. You know we needed to sow our wild oats. No one bothered to tell us that if we sowed our seeds to the wind, we would reap our harvest in a whirlwind. With the onset of challenges along the way, sowing wild oats was no longer fun but now we had to face a new reality, we are no longer young adults. What happened to time?

My how time has slipped away.

Now we were adults wondering where has time gone? We discovered our entire life had passed us by. We failed to plan for our future. We have wandered so far away from the old traditions of God first. We have spent too much time feeding our flesh. Now flesh is not so exciting, but I thought I had so much time.

We are now in the fall of our lives and we are acutely aware that we have wasted our time. There is no Garden called Beautiful in our realm. Happiness is illusive and it comes from within when we have a relationship with God. We can never be happy with someone else until we find peace within our own soul. Love is a river that flows from within. There is no happiness without the love of God. There is no love, until you know intimacy with yourself. INTO ME SEE equals intimacy, looking deep inside yourself and knowing yourself, loving yourself and having a personal relationship your maker is true intimacy. Once you know yourself and have an intimate relationship with Christ, the inner longing for love from someone else ceases.

Life's Situations

When I look at life's situations, I know they will not last.

I have the calm assurance; this too shall pass.

This is like a place on the road of life,

Some places are filled with joy; others are filled with strife.

If we could choose all the places we would see or be,

We would all be joyful; there would no misery!

Each new day brings it's own surprises and lessons,

If we would learn from them, they will be remembered as blessings!

"Lord Help Me Find My Way"

Like a ship that is lost at sea,

I am in life's storm. Lord please rescue me.

I feel battered and beaten by waves of situations.

Often feeling trapped, making mistakes in desperation.

Lord help me find my way is my cry.

If the water overflows my soul, I will surely die!

Lord help me find my way is ever my plea.

I am shipwrecked on an island called Despair; please rescue me.

Prayer after prayer is my call in distress.

I will hold to the saying, God knows what is best.

With the moon shining by night and the sun shining by day,

I feel New Hope in the Lord showing me the way.

***Then hear thou in heaven, and forgive the sin of thy servants, and of thy people Israel, that thou teach them the good way wherein they should walk, and give rain upon thy land, which thou hast given to thy people for an inheritance. *1 Kings 8:36 KJV*

*+

Mr. Nondescript

There was a man, that finally slipped,

He called himself Mr. Nondescript.

He was an infidel that was without conscious, he was very cold,

He wasn't discreet; in fact he was all too bold.

He did not have respect for himself or his home,

He allowed his lover to enter his residence while his wife was gone.

He was a very cunning man you must know,

He was a master deceiver who had clearly done this before.

He was a predator, who claimed to be victimized by life,

In fact the true victims were his lovers and his wife.

Being tactless was a common thing for him to do,

He was so full of himself, until he thought his own lies were true.

He had become separated from God along the way,

Even though he attended church routinely every Sunday.

He was a man of absolute routines,

His religion was just another part of his mad schemes.

Some people go to church to worship God and pray,

Church was another place he had picked up women to play.

He never realized that God frowns on people playing church,

Until he became ill and felt the Master's touch.

Is there any wonder that he finally slipped?

He forgot God is in control of everyone, including Mr. Nondescript.

My Dream Last Night

The dream was vivid and very long.
There was a king and there was a throne.
As I walked in this strange place,
With the king and his men I came face to face.
They took me to a far away place
Then the king vanished without a trace.
Many days and nights went by,
I would sit alone and cry.
Why did he bring me to this place?
Then disappeared without a trace.
I would sit in my lonely space,
I would try hard to see his face.
I would search and search in the corners of my mind,
No matter how I searched I could not find.
The king who brought me to this place,
Then disappeared without a trace.
After many years had gone by
He returned and I wondered why.
He said to me, your time here has come to an end.
I said to him, where shall I go? How do I begin?
I had to return to a place that I called home.

I was older now; I'd be alone.

This is the essence of my dream,

A common woman who met a king!

My Girls

My daughters are very, very precious to me.

I have learned not to comment on how they live their lives; I let them be free.

They are free to choose the path they will take.

I trust they will turn to the Comforter before their hearts begin to break.

I know that I have a special place in each one's life.

I encourage them to keep the faith and trust in Christ.

Each one is very unique and strong.

Each one a woman of faith that teaches her children right from wrong.

I ask the Comforter to give them what they need each day.

I taught them to put on the full armor of God each day when they pray.

When I think of all the prayers I could say;

I pray that they walk as godly women and bless others along life's way.

Inspired by Celestine & Catrina

“My Journey along the Bottom of the Sea”

This was a very strange dream to me,

It took me to the bottom of the sea!

The method of transport was so bizarre!

You would never guess; I was driving a car!

The adventure started on the shore,

Before I knew it I was on the sea’s floor.

This all seemed so bizarre to me

Driving a car on the bottom of the sea.

The top of the car was made of glass,

I could see many creatures and fishes as they passed.

I was so amazed at what I could see.

I was baffled by this journey under the sea.

I drove for miles and miles it seemed.

I kept telling myself, “it is just a dream.”

I began to think, “is this a lost world?”

My head was full of questions then it began to swirl!

After awhile I saw rays of light from the sun,

Then I knew my journey had just begun.

I came on shore in some strange land,

The plants were tropical; there was pure white sand.

The natives there seemed familiar to me.

I thought to myself, “how could this be?”

After my car stopped I opened the door.

I wondered to myself, "have I been here before?"

This all started with a journey under the sea,

Now these natives are saying they know me.

They got my clothing from the car,

I needed to change; I have journeyed so far.

They want me to rest for now,

Then tomorrow I will tell them how.

This all started so strange for me,

It was my journey under the sea.

"No Reason to Lie!"

There is no reason to tell a lie.

A lack of courage can cause you to cry.

Once you lie, you become ashamed,

Your days and nights are never the same.

You have to remember every lie you have told,

Now you have entered the battle for your soul.

There is no such thing as an innocent lie,

It's the loss of innocence that will cause you to die!

The serpent lied to Eve in the Garden,

Now we must pray to the Savior to be pardoned.

There is no reason to tell a lie,

If you listen, I will tell you why.

If you repent, you will be forgiven.

God gave us a gift that will keep on giving.

Trust in God and believe what I say is true,

Open your heart to receive is all you need to do!

"Please Comfort Me"

When my heart is sore with pain,

I feel I am alone and fear I will go insane.

I am so sad and I wonder why?

I no longer want to live, I say I want to die.

A voice from within says, I must live and not die.

I need to face the truth and rebuke the lie.

I now walk in a world full of delusions.

I cannot determine if this is real or an illusion.

I am bewildered and not free.

I must still remember to ask the Savior to comfort me.

Please comfort me I pray.

I somehow strayed along the way.

No peace or pleasure can I find?

I can no longer live chained and bound.

My prayer is to be free,

Please Jesus, Comfort me!

Thou art my hiding place and my shield;
I hope in thy word. Psalms 119:114 KJV

Inspired by the chained and bound

Please Hold Me in Your Arms

Lord, I don't want to be alone.

Please will you shelter me and make me strong?

I have made so many mistakes in the past,

I was in and out of relationships that just didn't last.

Please hold me in your arms,

I really need a shelter from life's storms.

I want you to guide me as each new day begins.

Please direct every aspect of my life, even selecting my friends.

Hold me in your arms is my plea forever more.

In the shelter of your arms I will be safe as never before.

Have not I commanded thee? Be strong and be of good courage; be not afraid, neither be thou dismayed; for the Lord thy God is with thee whithersoever thou goest. Joshua 1:9KJV

Please Show Me The Way

Lord, I have spent so much time going astray,

I must admit that I am lost; show me the way.

A sense of urgency is bearing down on me,

Please open my eyes so I can see.

Spiritual blindness has taken my sight,

I have stumbled through my days as though they were nights.

I ate the world's dainties with foolish delight.

I did not try to resist; I enjoyed every bite.

Then all of a sudden there was an awakening in me,

I realized I was lost and I could not see.

I could no longer find my own way,

I could not speak; I had nothing to say.

I found myself down and in great despair,

My soul cried out...Lord are you there?

Something awful has gotten a hold on me,

I need you Dear Lord to set me free.

I have faltered and fallen deep into sin,

I am seeking restoration so I can live again.

Like a lost sheep I've gone astray,

Lord you are the Good Shepherd, Please Show Me The Way.

Pretending To Give

You came to me as a bearer of gifts,

I knew in my spirit your heart would shift.

You would say with your mouth, "I love you",

But the Comforter kept telling me your words were not true.

I had a question about your giving within myself,

Why give a gift and tell everyone else?

A gift from the heart is given in privacy,

You don't need public accolades, just thanks to you from me.

A gift is always given from the heart,

The spirit in which it is given never departs.

The true bearer of a gift would never ask for the present back,

If this is done, why pretend? It's all just an act.

So if a bearer of gifts ever does this to you,

This is a sign of an unstable mind that cannot be true.

The Bearer of Gifts likes Pretending To Give to his fellowman,

Never take his instability personal, even he doesn't understand.

Secrets from the Well-Spring of Your Soul

Life long memories are given to the subconscious mind to keep,

They are sometimes unpleasant and cause loss of sleep.

As time passes by, the secrets begin to unfold,

They were once very deep in the Well-Spring of Your Soul.

Secrets from the Well-Spring start to overflow,

You wonder if it was a dream or it really happened long ago.

You begin to search in the corners of your mind,

The answers to these dreams you may not find.

Secrets are just deceptions that you want to hide,

You trust the subconscious mind to keep buried deep inside.

You never thought that a flood in your life would cause an overflow,

Memories that were hidden are not secrets any more.

The floodgates of your mind are opened and secrets begin to seep,

They are no longer hidden for your subconscious to keep.

Now From The well-spring of your soul,

Many, many secrets flow that were never told.

Someone Is Watching Over Me

There are times when I think no one can see,

Yet I know in my heart someone is watching over me.

It doesn't matter about the trials that come during the day,

I never get discouraged; I know that relief is just a prayer away.

I know that God's love truly abounds,

I find strength in his promises whenever I'm feeling down.

I know that his love is like a fountain that overflows,

I can drink the healing waters that God so freely pours.

I know God is with me even though I cannot see his face,

It is the power of his presence that keeps me in a peaceful space.

God is always with me even when things go wrong.

He promised to carry me when I'm too weak to go on.

There are times when I am as lonely as one can be,

I find comfort in knowing; Someone Is Watching Over Me.

Stop Looking Back

You can stop looking back at yesterday's pains,

The sting should be gone; it's only the memories that remain.

Why become a prisoner of what used to be,

The shackles have been broken; you've been set free.

I know that you had been bound for so long,

Until you could not remember that your shackles are gone.

You must first experience freedom in your mind,

If you do not... you will still remain mentally bound.

You see, even through the shackles are long gone,

The tormenting memories replay in your mind like a sad song.

Revisiting yesterday's wounds only causes you pain,

Like a devourer it destroys everything you have obtained.

There is but one way to find relief,

Give this burden to Jesus who bears all our grief.

This is a battle that you can win,

But you must give those thoughts to Jesus again and again.

Like a phantom the memories haunt you from day to day,

Whenever the memories reoccur, you should start to pray.

Then before you know it the painful phantom will go away,

You can Stop Looking Back and live in hope of a better day!

Be careful for nothing; but in every thing by prayer and supplication with thanksgiving let your requests be made known unto God. 7] And the peace of God, which passeth all understanding, shall keep your hearts and mind through Christ Jesus. Philippians 4:6-7 KJV

Let all bitterness, and wrath, and anger, and clamor, and evil speaking, be put away from you, with all malice. 32] And be ye kind to one another; tenderhearted, forgiving one another, even as God for Christ's sake hath forgiven you. Ephesians 4:31-32 KJV

"Taking Life in Stride"

Taking life in stride is the call of the day,

You must first seek the Comforter's will no matter how you pray.

For it is the will of God that really has true meaning

He is that strong tower on which we are constantly leaning.

So remember when you attempt to take life in stride,

You must rid yourself of false self- pride!

False self -pride can only cause a great fall,

You'll find yourself face to face with the fact that you need God after all.

So whenever self starts to get in the way,

Remember; give thanks to the Provider of all your needs as you pray.

The Dawning of a New Day!

With the dawning of this day,

I look to heaven and begin to pray.

I thank my God for sparing my life,

I will focus on the good and tell him about my strife.

When the load is too hard for me to bear,

I go into my secret closet for intimate prayer.

I know I can leave all my burdens with Him,

Even when to others… hope seems dim.

My Savior is the ultimate power on earth,

He is the only way for spiritual rebirth.

With spiritual rebirth I have found,

I can look to Him and never look down!

He can do what no other power can do.

You can search your whole life through.

To you my friend I would like to share,

The inner healing power of prayer!

The Day You Were Born!

For Steven Jay

The day you were born started out bright.
My contractions started in the middle of the night!
I lay on my bed all night long,
I knew in my heart that I had to be strong!
Your brother and sister lay sleep on their beds,
While many thoughts ran through my head.
I called your grandparents late at night,
If they did not come, it would not seem right.
I knew I could not wait long to phone,
I could not leave your siblings at home alone.
It was the last few hours that I wanted to pace,
Then I went to the hospital with my suitcase.
I knew the time was near,
No time for screaming! No time for tears!
This was not an easy task,
But I knew in my heart the pain would not last.
So at 7:33AM,
My son was born! Very fair skinned!

The Hated One

From the very moment you announced that you could love two,
I had a complete understanding of how I had been despised by you.
For it is written that no man can serve two gods,
Any such declaration causes division in his heart.
He will never treat both his lovers the same,
He will lift one high upon a pedestal; the other he will treat with disdain.
I cannot forget your reaction when I just called your name,
Anything was a reason for anger; you always had reasons to blame.
Now I sit and I wonder why I held onto you for all these years,
But I have learned so many lessons through tribulations and tears.
As I look to God who created everything under the sun,
I ask for wisdom and understanding about being The Hated One.
How can someone who says that they love you treat you so bad?
They push to the breaking point; sometimes you think you're going mad.
There were times when I thought I'd lose my mind,
Just pleading and asking God, how could anyone He made be so unkind?
But I knew in my heart there was a great lesson in it all, just for me,
Being the Hated One nearly destroyed me, yet it set me free.

No one can serve two masters; for either he will hate the one and love the other, or else he will be loyal to the one and despise the other. You cannot serve God and Mammon. (riches) Matthew 6:24 *NKJV*

The Rope of Hope

When the tides of life begin to come in,

You may feel abandoned by those you once called your friends.

The tides of life are the circumstances that flood your soul,

When you've been trying hard to overcome and reach your goals.

Then you realize that you cannot make this journey alone,

You have become weak; you cannot find the strength within yourself to go on.

You are so weary until you're holding onto life by a thread,

You realize you need a Savior; your soul needs to be fed.

You heard someone say, "if you just hold on and try to cope,

The Savior will come to cast out The Rope of Hope.

You must reach beyond what and where you can see,

You must believe the Savior is going to deliver you and set you free.

There is no reason for you to fear or doubt,

You can reach beyond the break and the Savior will pull you out.

Like an illusive phantom the shadows of depression begins to creep in,

You tell yourself there is hope for tomorrow and you can begin again.

You think about the many ways that you can cope,

In reality there is but one way; it's the Savior who extends The Rope of Hope.

As you reach beyond the break to hold on,

You can hear the Savior saying, "my child I am your strength be strong."

The Rope of Hope is strong enough to withstand the tides of life,

When you reach beyond what you can see, there is restoration from pain and strife.

But sanctify the Lord God in your hearts: and be ready always to give an answer to every man that asketh you a reason of the hope that is in you with meekness and fear. 16] Having a good conscience; that, whereas they speak evil of you, as of evildoers, they may be ashamed that falsely accuse your good conversation in Christ. 17] For it is better, if the will of God be so, that ye suffer for well doing, than for evil doing. 1 Peter 3:15-17 KJV

The Seasons of Life Will End

You will go through so many changes everyday,

These changes form the seasons in your life that will pass away.

You may think that life's seasons sound a little strange,

But your life like the earth has seasons that will surely change.

There were times when I've watched children at play,

Before I knew it they were all grown –up; time had slipped away.

Now I can see teenagers thirsting for life,

Making unsound decisions that may cause them strife.

Then come the young adults who will no longer play,

They're energetic and creative, trying to find their way.

These are the high achievers; they've obtained a reasonable amount of success.

They are fast approaching the fall of their life; they want less stress.

Oh me! Oh my! They say; "where has time gone"?

It seems like just yesterday when they wanted to be grown.

Looking back over their lives inventorying their achievements along the way,

Now they're contemplating the golden years asking, "was the price too high to pay"?

Should've, would've, could've are now their closest friends,

They're now lamenting the way they've lived their life, wanting to live it over again.

Then someone cried out to God, "Please help me find my way,

I'm sorry I didn't get to know you better, please teach me to pray"?Now you're asking God to forgive you for not spending more time with your family and friends,

You must now cope with reality; you are almost at life's end.

Again someone called out to God saying, "I should've spent time with you"!

Now that my life is almost over …tell me what shall I do?

My God please, don't let it be too late,

Please restore the joy of thy salvation for my own sake?

Before my silver cord is broken, please help me make amends,

Please my Heavenly Father, forgive me for my sins?

I am acutely aware that The Seasons of Life Will End,

Please learn to live life well... for you like me shall never walk this way again.

Create in me a clean heart, O God; and renew a right spirit within me. 11] Cast me not away from thy presence; and take not thy Holy Spirit from me. 12] Restore unto me the joy of thy salvation; and up hold me with thy free spirit. Psalm 51: 10-12 KJV

"The Stranger in My Bed"

A Spiritually Bankrupt person

Who is this man in my bed?

I can hear that thought resounding in my head!

He seems so familiar to me,

Yet I say, "how can this be?"

He lays there, distant and cold.

He is not my husband; he is just a vacant soul.

Who is this man in my bed?

The thought keeps resounding in my head!

I keep asking myself, "how can this be?"

This man is in bondage; he is not free.

He lay there, night after night and pretends,

He doesn't talk; he doesn't know where to begin.

Who is this man in my bed?

He doesn't know; "I am sure he said!"

Is he my friend? Or could he be a foe?

I look at him and I still do not know.

He has caused me such pain and such dread,

"How can he live with himself?" I often said.

Who is this man in my bed?

The question replays in my head.

Time and time again,

I tell myself, "he is not my friend!"

Who is this man in my bed?

I think I know. He is the living dead!

Nevertheless, to avoid fornication, let every man have his own wife, and let every woman have her own husband.3] Let the husband render unto his wife due benevolence: and like wise also the wife unto her husband. 4] The wife hath not power of her own body, but the husband: and likewise also the husband hath no power of his own body, but the wife.
5] Defraud ye not one the other, except it be with consent for a time that ye may give yourselves to fasting and prayer; and come together again, that satan tempt you not for your incontinency. 1 Corinthians 7:2-4 KJV

The Things I Know

There are so many things I know.

I look at life as never before.

I would like to say I have lived life well,

But as you know it has been hell.

I have had my share of happy times,

I should rejoice and say, life has been fine.

But like most people I know,

I don't aim high ...I just shoot low.

There are many wonderful things in life,

I will focus more on them and focus less on strife.

I will just say to my mind... be still,

Then I will always seek God's will.

There are so many wonderful places to go.

Places and things I have never seen before.

For HE THAT WILL LOVE LIFE, AND SEE GOOD DAYS, LET HIM REFRAIN HIS TONGUE FROM EVIL, AND HIS LIPS THAT THEY SPEAK NO GUILE. 11] LET HIM ESCHEW EVIL, AND DO GOOD; LET HIM SEEK PEACE, AND ENSUE IT. 12] FOR THE EYES OF THE LORD ARE OVER THE RIGHTEOUS, AND HIS EARS ARE OPEN UNTO THEIR PRAYERS: BUT THE FACE OF THE LORD IS AGAINST THEM THAT DO EVIL. 1 Peter 3:10-12 KJV

The Wounded Child

The wounded child cries out again and again.
This child cannot comprehend all the agonizing pain.
The child is tormented day and night.
His world is full of anger and he wants to fight.
He knows that if he fights; he will not win.
He lives in bondage and wants to be free again.
The child asked, "Why am I in so much pain?"
No matter how I try nothing seems to change.
He sits and wonders; what did he do wrong?
He feels so helpless and says he cannot go on.
He knows he cannot surrender his life to sin.
He shouted Jesus! Where do I begin?
He fell on his knees and began to pray,
He cried Lord, "Please guide me in the right way".
I am your child, show me where to begin.
I want to be free from sadness and pain.
The more he prayed the wounds began to heal.
He was released from the pain he did not want to feel.
The weight of the world he would no longer bear,
He found relief through fervent prayer.

Inspired by Wounded children

Cease from anger, and forsake wrath: fret not thyself in any wise to do evil. Psalm 37:8 KJV

Beloved, think it not strange concerning the fiery trial which is to try you, as though some strange thing happened unto you. 13] But rejoice, inasmuch as ye are partakers of Christ's sufferings; that when his glory shall be revealed, ye may be glad also with exceeding joy.
1 Peter: 12-13 KJV

"Times When I Cannot Pray"

When my heart is heavy laden; I cannot seem to pray.

I ask the Holy Spirit to intercede for me and help me find my way.

There are times when situations in my life weigh me down,

I open my mouth to pray, but there are no sounds.

I now realize I have come to a dry place in my life.

The spring of hope has run dry and I wonder why?

A voice from within my soul whispered, "my child be still"!

Go to the fountain of living water where you can be refilled.

The water from that fountain is good for restoring your soul.

It flows from a land where you never ever grow old.

So when I am unable to pray and feel low.

I go to the fountain for atonement and to be filled to over flow.

True Love Is Divine

It has been said, "that true love is blind,

But I must say love covers a multitude of sins, it is divine".

As I lay in your arms I feel such love as we embrace,

I know these feelings are divine, they come from a higher place.

I truly believe that love is heaven sent,

Lust is here today gone today and you wonder where it went.

True love never dwindles like ice that melts,

After an encounter it doesn't make you wonder what is was you felt.

Its' not like the setting sun at the end of the day,

Love is eternal; it is here to stay.

Surely...True Love Is Divine,

It lives on and on in our hearts and minds.

For, brethren, ye have been called unto liberty; only use not liberty for an occasion to the flesh, but by love serve one another. 14] For all the law is fulfilled in one word, even in this; THOU SHALT LOVE THY NEIGHBOUR AS THYSELF. Galatians 5:13-14 KJV

Victimized Girl Child

A victimized girl child is never the same,

There is nothing you can do to take away the pain.

She looks inside herself and wondered what did she do?

She knew that the society would paint a picture that just wasn't true.

She began to wonder how could the world be so cold,

Man would take away her virtue to feed his own soul.

The girl looked to her parents for comfort and understanding,

Instead the parents reacted with questions that were dehumanizing and demanding.

The girl dies inside a little each day,

With no comfort from the parents the girl wants to run away.

The girl just wants her parents to hold her in their arms,

She is like a wounded bird that wants shelter from the storm.

Her parents cannot move beyond their own pain and false pride,

She begins to think; "it would have been better if she had died".

After all her parents would not need to feel ashamed,

They forgot that she was the victim whom society evidently blames.

This child will carry her wounds until her life ends,

Only God can restore her and make her whole again.

It is good to know that God's power is very great for those of us who believe and there is restoration and healing after victimization. After all, society often responds to a victim like she or he is the perpetrator of the crime that was against her or him.

Weaving The Tapestry Of Our Lives

As we live our lives a tapestry we weave,
God brings us in contact with so many people while many blessings we receive.
These people are the many threads that give our tapestry form.
They are the positive and negative contacts that we make from the time we're born.
The people who cross our paths are touched in a special way,
Sometimes an angelic being seemingly touches us; we begin to pray.
Our tapestry has a large legacy over the years,
Its' beauty includes periods of blessings, great joy, sorrow and tears.
There were many life lessons that were learned,
And periods of great spiritual awakening when our hearts just burned.
There were times when there was a yearning to be free,
We knew that repentance and restoration gave absolute liberty.
We knew in our hearts that we must answer the call,
Before our tapestry could be complete and hung on the wall.
Sometimes there were tears that had be to mended,
They were caused by life circumstances and the people we offended.
Complete restoration would bring the making of our tapestry to an end,
All we had to do was call Jesus; he forgave our every sin.
I knew we could find rest for our weary souls at Jesus' feet.
Our life's journey would be over once our tapestry is complete.

“What Does It Mean To Lose Your Mind?

How does a person lose his or her mind?

Once it is lost can it be found?

Where does the search for your mind begin or end.

Do you travel alone to search for your mind or with a friend?

It has been said that a loss of faith and hope is at the root of the mind taking flight.

A loss of faith and hope causes restless days and sleepless nights.

The thought of losing your mind causes unrelenting fear.

It may cause you to wonder if your time is near.

This unexplained flight of the mind,

Has created a search for answers that are hard to find.

Fear in great measure is not good.

It is from the deceiver and should be understood.

We live in a society under constant pressure.

We must remember having faith and hope decrease our daily stresses.

What does it mean to lose your mind?

The mind is lost when memories cannot be found.

Have not I commanded thee? Be strong and of a good courage; be not afraid, neither be thou dismayed: for the Lord thy God is with thee whithersoever thou goest. Joshua 1:9 KJV

What If

What if God had given His Son and taken Him back,

The world would be without hope and full of lack.

We would be at the mercy of ruthless men's greed and anger,

Those who believed would live in constant danger.

There would be no one to stand in our stay,

There would be no Christ to intercede for us when we pray.

Can you imagine a world without hope?

There would be no Master Plan and no way to cope.

If God had refused to permit His Son to die at Calvary,

Our world today would be full of anguish and misery.

There would be no hope of restoration; no redemption plan,

A world without a Savoir leaves no hope for mortal man.

I just shudder in fear to think...What If?

What if God had refused to give the world the Ultimate Gift?

What If?

Where and how would man spend eternity?

If Jesus had not died on Calvary.

There would be no hope for mortal man,

The world would be a dark place; oppressed by the evil one's hand.

Father, I want to thank you for giving the world the Ultimate Gift,

There is hope for the world; we don't have to wonder What If?

For God so loved the world that He gave his only begotten Son, that whosoever believeth in him should not perish, but have everlasting life. 17] For God sent not his Son into the world to condemn the world; but that the world through him might be saved. John 3:16-17 KJV

When Disappointment Lose Its Sting

When the pain of disappointment lose its sting;

You will let go of the past and start to dream.

There is hope for tomorrow you will say,

“I overcame my past wounds day by day”.

If you become a prisoner of your past,

You will journey through your life wearing a mask.

Holding on to the pain from yesterday,

Causes confusion and pain that will not go away.

You will know that disappointment has lost its’ sting;

When you stay out of the past and plan to fulfill your dreams.

"When Your Faith Grows Dim"

There are times when your faith grows dim.

Your heart is filled with anger and you no longer trust Him.

The real truth you will not speak;

You give it to the subconscious mind to keep.

What causes faith to lose its' glow?

Misplaced confidence in someone you love and know.

You start out blaming God for your problems,

When your heart is heavy laden, you run to Him to solve them.

Please remember before your faith grows dim,

The Comforter is with us, trust in Him.

"When I'm in the Shelter of His Arms"

When I'm in the shelter of His arms,

I am hidden and safe from harm.

There are times that I may fret.

I must remember God has never failed me yet!

Unlike man, God does not lie!

I can hold on to His promises and never cry.

He is my shelter in every storm,

He has promised to keep me from harm.

When trying situations come, I may be alarmed.

Then I think of the protection I have in the shelter of His arms.

Sometimes I look at the circumstances of a trying day!

I admit that I am powerless and begin to pray.

Lord put me in a place where I am safe from this storm.

Please hide me in the shelter of Your arms.

Inspired by a trying day!

Although the fig tree shall not blossom, neither shall fruit be in the vines; the labour of the olive shall fail, and the fields shall yield no meat; the flock shall be cut off from the fold, and there shall be no herd in the stalls: 18] Yet I will rejoice in the Lord, I will rejoice in the God of my salvation.
Habakkuk 3:17-18 KJV

When I Am Too Sick To Go On

I have become weak; I am no longer strong.

I feel too sick and weary to go on.

I hold on for my family and my friends,

They cannot cope with my journey coming to an end.

I need them to accept that I must go.

My journey here is over; earth is not my home anymore.

Life and love has been very good to me.

I had a full life, now my spirit wants to be set free.

I can leave now, with no regrets.

I shall live on in the memories of those who choose never to forget.

I want you to live encouraged for this is not the end.

If you trust and believe in Jesus, we shall meet again.

And many of them that sleep in the dust of the earth shall awake, some to everlasting life, and some to shame and everlasting contempt. 3] And they that be wise shall shine as the brightness of the firmament; and they that turn many to righteousness as the stars forever and ever.
Daniel 12:2-3 KJV

When I Have Traveled the Last Mile

When I have traveled the last mile;

I will answer the call, “come home my child”.

I have endured many heartbreaks and snares.

My soul has taken wings to meet Jesus in the air.

I was blest by so many friends along the way;

I must leave them behind until the end of their days.

There is no occasion for sadness or tears.

I had my share of blessings through the years.

I know my friends will miss me but I just had to go!

My journey had ended in this world below.

I felt so lonely and so depressed.

I heard the voice of Jesus say, “come unto me I will give you rest”.

I could no longer tarry in this world where I felt so alone.

I decided to leave this world behind and make heaven my home.

Inspired by the Honey Bunny

Yea, though I walk through the valley of the shadow of death, I will fear no evil: for thou art with me; thy rod and thy staff they comfort me.
Psalm 23:4 KJV

"When Love Lets You Down"

When love, as you know it, let's you down,

You stop being happy and start to frown.

This is not a reason to stop living,

You have a heart full of love; you can keep on giving.

You must hold your head up high,

Never let true love pass you by.

Or you will live life with regrets,

Holding on to memories you will never forget.

There are a few questions that you must ask.

If it was love, why didn't it last?

Take time to ponder all of the facts,

Stay in the present. Don't look back.

Then at your life's journey end,

You can say I had true love; I loved my family and friends.

"When Trouble Comes To Your Door"

When trouble comes to your door,

You experience more grief than ever before.

Day and night you wonder why?

Instead of praying, you start to cry.

Once the door is opened, the warfare begins!

You wonder what happened to your family and your friends!

You begin to sink into the valley of despair,

Then you begin to wonder does anyone really care?

Now you have fallen into the pit of depression,

You are unaware this could be spiritual oppression!

The burden becomes more than you can bear,

Then you think, "what I really need is prayer!"

As you lay your head on your pillow to rest,

A soft voice whispers, "your burdens will be less."

There are no burdens that Jesus cannot bear.

You have the calm assurance that He really cares.

“When Trouble Comes Your Way”

Your prayer is for plenty of grace for the day,

Your list grows longer as you continue to pray.

You look over your life and see God’s grace in overflow.

You begin to thank God and your faith begins to grow.

When you are faced with the evils of each new day,

You must get on your knees and begin to pray.

You know God will give you a sanctuary from harm,

If you ask, He will hide you in the shelter of His arms.

You know what to do, When Trouble Comes Your Way,

Lift your heart toward heaven; then bow your head and pray.

When Wolves Hide In The House of God

When wolves come to the House of God to hide,

They put on Sheep's Clothing and cause havoc inside.

Their hearts were full of evil from the day they were born,

They are as seductive as a pied piper with a horn.

They come to entice, mislead, destroy and to kill.

They are evil and have no veneration for God's Will.

People do not realize that they are princes of the air,

They are destroyers and they do not revere the Lord's Prayer.

If ever a wolf would pray for transformation of his awful state,

His heart would be transformed and evil would dissipate.

The Church of God must speak out against all that is not of God.

Especially if there has been deception in a leader's heart!

Ye shall walk after the Lord your God, and fear Him, and keep his commandments, and obey his voice, and ye shall serve him, and cleave unto him. Deuteronomy 13:5 KJV

And I say also unto thee,That thou art Peter, and upon this rock I will build my church; and the gates of hell shall not prevail against it.
Matt.16: 18 KJV

"When You Cannot Sleep At Night"

There are times you cannot sleep at night.

The burdens of the day makes sleep take flight.

The voice of the accuser whispers…no one cares.

Your heart becomes troubled and sleep vanishes into the air.

You toss and turn all night.

You know what you are hearing doesn't sound right.

You awake in the morning, tired as can be.

Your heart is heavy laden…you are no longer at peace.

Your soul cries out, this is too much to bear!

You will find relief in fervent prayer.

Now at the close of an exhausting day;

You found the answer you began to pray.

When you cannot sleep at night;

Fervent prayer makes everything all right.

"When you feel you cannot go on"

There are times when you feel you cannot go on.

You feel burdened and oppressed by life's storms.

You enter into a world of defeat and despair,

You tell yourself, your burdens are too hard to bear.

Your faith has dwindled and you feel very weak.

You are tired and confused from a lack of sleep.

You go through your day with your heart heavy and walking in a daze.

You are unable to pray and count your blessings or sing songs of praise.

You keep thinking you cannot go on.

A voice from within whispers my child, just be strong.

I am renewing you for the challenges of life that will come your way,

Hold on to your faith; His grace is sufficient to take you through the day.

So, when you feel you cannot go on;

Praying and believing is the key to making those without hope strong.

Inspired by those without Hope

"When You Think No One Cares"

You are sometimes in a desert in your life.

Your spirit is wounded and your heart is full of pain and strife.

Like an island, you feel alone.

You feel down and abandoned. All hope is gone.

When you enter the garden of despair,

You wander aimlessly; telling yourself no one cares.

You seem to wander deeper and deeper into this garden.

You are held captive until you learn to forgive and pardon.

In this garden there is a valley called dry bones,

You keep revisiting the valley until you feel more alone.

In the valley your faith and hope takes flight.

Negative thoughts echo in your mind day and night.

While in the valley you lose all hope and become filled with despair.

You keep telling yourself no one really cares.

The pain you have endured has become our constant friend,

Change comes only if you choose to bring this journey in the garden to an end.

You have been here so long, holding onto the wounds of days gone by,

You will be free when the sting of the pain no longer makes you cry.

Spiritual renewal and restoration will bring this journey to an end

You will be free from past wounds and a new journey of faith and hope begins!

Inspired by those without Hope

"When You Walk Through Your Storm"

When you walk through your storm;

You will seek shelter from all harm.

You will wonder where your serenity has gone,

The skies are always gray there is no sun.

There will be no shelter to keep you warm,

While you are walking through your storm.

You will try to walk fast because it is cold.

The revelation of why you are in this storm starts to unfold.

You asked for understanding as time began to pass,

A soft voice whispered; "my child this won't last".

I want you to learn to live by faith everyday,

And stay out of the past; just trust and obey.

I said to my heart, "heart be still".

Now I am ready and willing to do the Master's will.

When You Worship The God Of Self

When you worship the god of self;

You cannot think of anyone else.

You go through life in a daze,

Thinking only of yourself and giving self-praise!

You are so blind that you cannot see,

Self has bound you and you are no longer free.

You climb the ladder of success,

You cannot remember that you are blest.

Now you say, "I made it on my own".

You have forgotten God blest you, you did not succeed alone.

For all self-worshippers who forget how they made and begin to fall,

Then they remember Jesus had blest them after all.

Now instead of saying, "they made it on their own,

They cry out they cannot continue their journey alone".

Now they cry out to the Savior, "please save me today"!

If you help me now I will never forget to pray.

A heavenly voice whispers, "Child I have heard your call".

Just remember I am your Father, I will always catch you when you fall.

Inspired by the Boastful and Proud

When Your Mate Betrays You

Betrayal has no respect of gender

When your mate betrays you, your world as you have known it stands still. Your inner being starts to quake, one turbulent shaking after the other. A million thoughts and accusations flood your very soul. You start to pick yourself apart with every cruel word your mate has ever spoken to you. Self- hate from the pits of hell attacks you at the core of your being. You have restless days and sleepless nights to look forward to. Your mind is merciless and replays every negative thought you can imagine over and over again. This all comes from the accuser. You must remember satan attacks us in our minds with tormenting thoughts. You are not the infidel and you must not punish yourself. Nothing justifies infidelity!

Never once have you considered that this is a character defect in him. You are saying to yourself all the things he has said to make himself feel guiltless. All the anger and rage you feel for that person, you turn it within and it is almost unbearable. You tell your family and friends and they say things that cause you to feel worst. Although this is not their intent, it happens. You sink into a pit of dark depression. You repress your anger for your partner and look at yourself.

Self is weak and defenseless and will not fight you back. Unlike the infidel whose tongue is sharper than a double edge sword and is waiting to slash you if you think about talking about the issues at hand. After all, he could never talk to you, so he elected to talk about you and put you down to someone he has sexual desires for. It is all part of a grand scheme to satisfy the flesh. You are an innocent pawn in this game of lust and self- fulfillment. He is out to serve the god of self - fulfillment. He has been handed over to the Spirit of Delusion. He has answered that inner voice that sounds so sweet. The voice said, “go out find yourself a lover”. Your wife does not understand your needs, nor does she give you pleasure anymore. His heart is turned from you in the twinkling of an eye. The moment he entertained doing wrong, the evil one was there, waiting to accommodate him. His journey into darkness begins. Nothing you can say or do will please him now. The more you try to get him to be intimate with you, the more distant he becomes. He is drunk on the wine of deception. He is consumed and is walking in a world of delusions. He now believes every good thing you do is bad and the evil that he is doing is good, after all how can such a pleasurable encounter be evil or bad? This person has convinced himself that what he is doing is not hurting anyone, least of all you. He is now spiritually blind and cannot see. He is stumbling in a world full of delusions of grandeur. He is so sure this is love, until he can tell you that he is capable of loving two women. Maybe this person is not capable of loving anyone and relies solely on feelings and passion.

How can you believe this person is capable of love? After all, he tells you I love you from time to time in a tone that has no passion in it at all. He is also telling his new- found lust that he loves her also. How can something that should be good and pure hurt so badly? Love is kind, giving, patient, tender, unselfish, and sacrificing. It should never hurt! We shake ourselves and wonder. When did the passion in our relationship die?

Then you realized that it had slipped away one excuse after the other. You count all the complaints of fatigue and headaches and reality starts to set in.

When your mate betrays you, you must give him to God. You must stay out of the cycle of trying to get him to understand your pain. You must reach beyond what you feel to deliverance from the bondage of sadness that you will succumb to if you focus on what has happened to you. For you are not the victim, unless you allow yourself to fall prey to an unforgiving heart. Then you become bound by the very sin that gave you no pleasure. For it was your mate that had the lover, not you. You must forgive and give them to the Holy Spirit. The Holy Spirit will heal your broken heart, will stand by you and make you strong, will right every wrong, will direct you and put you in a place where you feel no pain. You can say the battle is not yours, it is the Lord's. You do not have to think about getting even, let the Comforter take charge. This will fill your heart with peace.

Remember the battle we fight in life is not against what we can see, it is spiritual. So, whenever you hear a voice whispering in your ear, weigh what it is saying. If it is mocking you and tormenting you, it is not of God, rebuke it! Tell it the battle is not yours, it is the Lord's.

Avoid letting your mate pull you into discussions where he tries to justify what he has done. Stay focused on the fact that he made the choice to bring a third – party into your relationship that is meant for two people and God. Let him deal with his inner-war without you becoming part of that battle.

In your hour of despair go to God in prayer and His grace and mercy will comfort you. This is not an easy task to forgive and to heal from the hurt and pain. Know that it is possible with God. Without God you are angry, bitter and out of control. Depression and self - hatred is waiting for you if you do not look to the Lord for deliverance.

For if after they have escaped the pollutions of the world through the knowledge of the Lord and Savior Jesus Christ, they are again entangled therein, and overcome, the latter end is worse than the beginning. 21] For it had been better for them not to have known the way of righteousness, than, after have known it, to turn from the holy commandment delivered unto them. 22] But it is happened unto them according to the true proverb, THE DOG IS TURNED TO HIS OWN VOMIT AGAIN; and the sow that was washed to her wallowing in the mire. 2 Peter: 20-22 KJV

Blessed is he whose transgression is forgiven, whose sin is covered.2] Blessed is the man unto whom the Lord imputeth not iniquity, and in whose spirit there is no guile. Psalm 32:1-2 KJV

Who's The Prisoner?

Who's the prisoner or should I ask?

Are you holding onto injuries from your past?

Evil deeds said and done,

Gone are the days of laughter and fun.

The pain and the hurt you can't let go.

Who's the prisoner? Don't you know?

A heart full of unforgiveness puts you in chains.

Your heart is so heavy –laden, you can't move beyond your pain.

You must be determined to break the chains that have you shackled.

Unforgiveness is the enemy you must tackle!

You will choose between being bound or being free.

Forgiveness is not a question it is the key.

When asked who's the prisoner? You will reply.

Forgiveness is a must, or else I will surely die!

For we know Him that hath said, "VENGENCE BELONGETH UNTO ME; I WILL RECOMPENSE, saith the Lord." And again, THE LORD SHALL JUDGE HIS PEOPLE. Hebrews 10:30 KJV

“Why Am I So Depressed?”

I sit in a world of my own;

I now realize I am alone.

I didn’t want to get up and I didn’t want to get dressed.

Could it be that I am depressed?

The things that I once valued and worked hard to gain,

Have no real meaning, I have labored in vain.

Why am I depressed I keep asking myself?

When you lose your drive to attain, there is nothing left.

Could it be that my goals were all wrong?

Fulfillment from material things never lasts long.

I once thought I had the world on a string,

I bought clothes, cars and diamond rings.

Why am I depressed the question resounds in my head!

I think I know the answer; “my soul needs to be fed”.

There is a thirst and hunger in my soul,

It is filled as the mystery of depression starts to unfold.

Why am I depressed is no longer the question.

I am now traveling in a spiritual direction.

I am no longer alone, I can honestly say.

“I found the answer I started to pray”!

Why Do I Feel So Alone?

I walk in a world all my own.

I must concede I feel so alone.

Even when I am in a crowd,

I am so alone I want to hide.

No matter where I am I feel the same.

This feeling of loneliness remains unchanged.

The roads I have traveled in life have brought me to this end.

I feel abandoned by my family and my friends.

I look for the truth in the grand scheme of life.

I must admit I am the author of most of my strife.

Why do I feel so alone?

I sit and wonder where I went wrong.

I said, "I don't need anyone".

I can do whatever I want to have fun!

I thought I had the world on a string.

I made it on my own I don't need anything!

I became so self -sufficient I thought I did not need God.

Then one day, my whole world fell apart.

Like all that fall, I began to pray.

It was through true repentance that I found the way.

I do not feel alone anymore.

I trust my Savior more than ever before.

“Why Do You Talk Like That”?

Why do you talk like that?

Is it your imagination or is it a fact?

Why do you make such strange sounds?

Are you having fun or saying something profound?

Why do you talk like that I often wonder?

Are you insecure and often blunder?

All the wounds in your spirit seem to flow outward when you speak,

Purge your soul and the answers you will no longer seek.

Why do you talk like that?

Are you expressing yourself From The well-spring of Your Soul?

If this is true, all of life mysteries will unfold.

Inspired by my daughter Catrina

Wounded Souls

Why so many wounded souls?

It is a mystery from the days of old.

The wounded ones are not hard to find,

Their spirits are broken and their heads are down.

They live in bondage they are not free.

They live in constant fear and misery.

They are unaware that they are seeping at the seams.

They live in constant terror, like a bad dream.

You hear them ask, "Where is God"?

He never has done His part!

If He lives, why am I in pain?

Shackled and bound with nothing to gain!

Someone said, "this is not so"!

There are many things you must know.

First, you must be willing to change.

Learn to let go of the guilt and the shame.

Holding on to the past only brings pain.

You become imprisoned with nothing to gain.

Seek the complete healing that will last.

Look to the future; let go of the past.

Inspired by the walking wounded

Your Child Is In Pain

What lessons have you taught your child?

Have you taught your child to live in denial?

Where does hiding pain begin?

Does it start with cheating and lying to a friend?

It all starts quite innocently…don't you know?

We have all walked that way before.

Again…what lessons have you taught your child?

They learn to live in pain, while wearing a smile.

A child hiding pain is forever changed,

They're helpless and hopeless; their lives will never be the same.

Then you want to make the pain go away,

But guilt and shame is the price the child will pay.

What a horrible thing to do,

Making a child hide things that are ugly and untrue.

Even though the child has so much fun at play.

You wonder why the child acts out everyday,

Could it be you were deliberately blind and did not want to see?

Silently you blame yourself and others for the child's pain and misery.

This horrible pain has pierced the child's soul,

It must seep out even though it's been untold.

Pain hidden in a child will not stay,

It will be revealed without warning someday.

Your Graduation Day

It has been a long time coming it may seem,

Years of studying and planning to fulfill your dreams.

Now that the road that led to high school has come to an end.

You must find where the pathway to college begins.

"There will be no sound future without higher Ed".

You must remember these words I have said.

Whatever you do, never forget to trust in God.

He will direct your path and guide your heart.

Inspired by my grand daughter

Your Special Place

Just think about God's amazing grace,

He told me to tell you of your special place.

It is a place that is yours alone,

He will hide you there when all your strength is gone.

It is also a place of restoration and the days are bright and fair,

You can have peace of mind and live without a care.

Your Special Place is just for you,

He will take you from the pit to a palace if you are willing to go through.

You can live carefree everyday,

But you must learn to trust God completely; that's the only way.

You see, there maybe some crosses for you to bear,

But don't loose heart; just remember He'll be right there.

You must know that as you journey along the way,

Always hold fast to your faith, no matter what anyone has to say.

There will be trials and tribulations from time to time,

But they come to make you ready and sound.

Your Special Place is in the heart of God,

And there is no power on earth that can tear you apart.

You have free will; so you can tell Him to go away,

Just remember there is no life where God does not stay.

And the Lord shall guide thee continually, and satisfy thy soul in drought, and make fat thy bones: and thou shalt be like a watered garden, and like a spring of water, whose waters fail not. Isaiah 58:11 KJV

Your Work Is Not Done!

There was a time they said you would die!
Then a voice from heaven answered my cry.
I heard the voice say, "her work is not done.
I have to make her ready for the race she must run".
As I sat by your bed day and night;
I knew you'd get stronger for the battle you must fight.
I held on to the promise that your work was not done.
I thought about the days when you laughed and had fun.
Then one day you awakened from the coma that had you bound to your bed.
I remembered every word the voice from heaven had said.
"Your work is not done there is a battle you must fight".
Then we discovered the first battle was to regain your sight.
We were in for a greater heartbreak,
The loss of your memory was hard for you to take.
I went to my prayer closet for fervent prayer,
I knew that there was healing oil there.
I was told as a child that it was good for the healing of a nation.
I asked the Lord, "heal my child your precious creation".
Again I heard the voice say, "her work is not done".
I am restoring her for the race she must run!

Inspired by my baby, Catrina

About The Author

Evelyn Dumas' Chavez was born in Waynesboro, Georgia. She started to write poetry in the fall of her life after a divine awakening. She and her husband, Robert have six children and numerous grandchildren and two great grandsons. They live in the cozy suburbs of a desert town in the Pacific Northwest. Her childhood passion was to become a minister. The very idea was troubling to her parents because it was not acceptable for girls of her time to become ministers. So she was always labeled as a people person, one who is able to console and listen to others. In her great love for God and people she would send cards and letters of comfort and encouragement.